From Other Tongues

poems by

Mary Strong Jackson

Finishing Line Press
Georgetown, Kentucky

From Other Tongues

Copyright © 2017 by Mary Strong Jackson
ISBN 978-1-63534-237-6 First Edition
All rights reserved under International and Pan-American Copyright Conventions.
No part of this book may be reproduced in any manner whatsoever without written permission from the publisher, except in the case of brief quotations embodied in critical articles and reviews.

ACKNOWLEDGMENTS

Litost: Published online by *The Mill*, millwriters.org, Appleton, WI 2016

Publisher: Leah Maines

Editor: Christen Kincaid

Cover Art: Nicholas Krauter, Mary Pattavina

Author Photo: Kathryn Krauter

Cover Design: Elizabeth Maines McCleavy

Printed in the USA on acid-free paper.
Order online: www.finishinglinepress.com
also available on amazon.com

Author inquiries and mail orders:
Finishing Line Press
P. O. Box 1626
Georgetown, Kentucky 40324
U. S. A.

Table of Contents

Petrichor   1

Torschlusspanik   2

Iksaurpok   3

Litost   4

Ya'aburnee   5

Sehnsucht   6

Cafuné   7

Jayus   8

Komorebi   9

L'appel du vide   10

Culaccino   11

Duende   12

Nefelibata   13

Querencia   15

Sobremesa   16

Svaha   17

Tingo   18

Glossary of Titles   19

About the Author   21

For Mya and Alex

This collection was inspired by words considered untranslatable into English with the exception of the poem, "Petrichor" which is a word coined in 1964 by Australian scientists. A glossary of the foreign words follows the final poem.

Petrichor

two gods
one made of stone
the other water
her water infuses him

she circles his body
like a river around rocks
his dense form leans
then lifts to greet her waves

giving her a solid sway
this is how rain meets the earth
how earth meets the rain
how a scent rises on the inhale

after water touches soil between stone
this ancient consilience
moves the mouths of mortals

to say "I love the smell of rain"

Torschlusspanik

years I lived without ravens
without their reminders
to ignore cautions
release my lungs
ease that nameless pining
that worries for answers
and forgets to fly

once a teacher
gave me a book
with the lines,
"Make no mistake. Everything
in the mind is in rat's country.
It doesn't die…you will only find
bits and cry out
because they were yourself."

but what of the bits
I never find
the lines in books no one shows me

how will I live with only one life
and this gate-closing panic

Iktsuarpok

she goes outside to see if anyone is coming
and every time she goes, the dog rises with her
weather is let in time and again
she goes out into the light
she goes out in darkness

to see if anyone is coming

she knows two things for sure—different animals hunt at night
hearts loosen in the chest when the sun drops

she hears scratching at her door
and opens it to see who's come
it's the dog or sometimes the calico cat
but she knows it might be miners clawing
their way to breath or that father of three delivering pizza
she hears his children singing for their supper
he hears them too
she sees it in his eyes

she goes out to see how faraway tomorrow is
to wonder what dreams will come
howls of wolves crawl her spine
she waits till shivers make her cross
back inside across the threshold
worn shiny by worry
looking first to see

if anyone is coming

each morning she looks for someone
then at the hill across the way
to see if its top is boiling
to see if lava runs down the hillside
though it never has, but she checks
because she feels heat rising up her legs

Litost

she'd caught sight of it
in shadows like a mouse
along the baseboards

but this
wanted her to see
and scurried less
seemed larger than before
she felt an unveiling coming
a reckoning
so she held a heavy blanket
one moonlit night and caught it

it had body and weight
afraid to unwrap it
but feeling she must
she laid the heavy thing on the bed
unwrapped it at snail's speed
making her bones ache with effort
felt a clawing under her skin

once unwrapped
it spelled out
words
each letter carved
from parts of her
soot   grime   boils
and blood
road rash and ringworms

she folded the blanket around it
held it against her offered warm tea
and rubbed it with oil to soften each part that protruded
whispered that mistakes could be rounded away from sharpness
and there would be no more dark scurrying

Ya'aburnee

not between cottonwoods and jack pines
bury me between your shoulder blades
where wild roots and twisted branches grow
bury me in the crook of your elbow
in the spirals of your ears

not on the broad-backed prairie
bury me behind your knees
under your tongue
in the hollow of your hip

don't bury me with dead spirits
put me in the musk-pit of your arm
the whorl of your belly-button
the sockets of both eyes
    bury me in your brain

Sehnsucht

the river padding against stone
sounds like footsteps beside her

she stops and listens again and again
as the sun breaks through billowy clouds

casting lines of light
in what her friend calls a God-sky

once she drove into a place
of old trees where she bought a house

now longing sits on the hearth beside her cat
even though she doesn't have a hearth

the leather of her shoes curved
and loosened fits around her odd little toes

she considers that these kinds of comforts
abound if only she might recognize them

is it the doorstep's broken corner of tile
that reminds to add not subtract love

or a collective yearning for nourishment
present at birth—searching for the nipple—

thousands and thousands of years
millions of yearners wrapping time

around each changing moment
she wakes one day   and for one moment

realizes   she's longing
for what she already has

Cafuné

his fingers breathed
murmurs of silent syllables

silky "esses"   caressing "cees"
through her hair

Jayus

accidents happen
closest to home
one last orange blossom beer
and the stoop's last step
twists your ankle
on what's supposed to be the landing

turns out home is for sloppy punchlines
ill-timed quick jabs and sideway
glances that slip down the wrong-way
you forget the pause
the one that leaves the audience hanging

off start beginnings—you slept with who?
confused middles—maybe if you just bought a red convertible
quick endings—grandma died at the casino in Deadwood

you can't help but laugh
as the oops-timed baby
coos up at you with eyes like stars

Komorebi

there is a wren's breath of silence
when a herd's last hoof comes to rest
and dust drifts back to the ground

this same kind of quiet beckons a body
to become a bit of flotsam
filtering through trees in a sunbeam

to nearly escape in silence
and light is enough
to succeed is sublime

L'appel du vide

he left a piece of dead bird
inside   inherited
he'd always been able
to get out of anywhere
or so he said
maybe through wood steel or stone
things that can be cut or busted

he never seemed to enter
inner places to test his theory
but how does one know
if another enters their own
dark nests of self
to face shriveled worms
that can't be stomached
or hollow bones of ancestors

I've seen ants crawling
over dead birds
if you dig into those place
it's more than handed-down myopia
it means figuring out if you're
a scavenger or the scavenged
each with a reason for being

it takes a jump from high places
I wish you'd jumped
not all birds get eaten by ants

Culaccino

once
it was you
alive and well
placing your glass down
at this corner table

its cool condensation
against your palm
made you think of the last night's fog
and the sound glasses make
when they touch

this day
a long-legged whiskey and coke drinker
sits at the table you always chose
maybe he was a whiskey and coke
she wonders and positions
her glass over your silvery circle
on this wooden pub table

Duende

After spending my quarter at Ralph's Jumble Shop,
I spoke to a parrot name Ruby
in a bar window in Chadron, Nebraska.
I was sent for stomach pills
after Grace drank too much
and came naked down the staircase
at the Hub Bar, while I sat
on a bar stool next to my dad.
Grace was my small town's "Nude
Descending a Staircase".
I knelt beside mother at mass,
found art in crisscrossed wrinkles
of old men's necks, while summer heat made
mirages on paved country roads.

Mirages on paved country roads
of old men's necks while summer heat made
found art in crisscrossed wrinkles.
I knelt beside mother at mass.
Descending a staircase,
Grace was my small town's nude
on a bar stool next to my dad
at the Hub Bar, while I sat
and came naked down the staircase.
After Grace drank too much,
I was sent for stomach pills.
In a bar window in Chadron, Nebraska,
I spoke to a parrot named Ruby
after spending my quarter in Ralph's Jumble Shop.

Nefelibata

at four months
she twisted her body
into a question mark
making it roll to one side
where she could see
the flowered pants of her aunt

she reached to touch the beginning
of her head-in-the-clouds-life
through fabric or forest no matter
if trees grew in her mind or her feet felt
mossy ground between bark bodies
she could go into crevices of wonder like a lost Alice

for years she spoke only to dogs
not many knew what she held inside
but before others noticed her absences of eons
and vast expanses her mother would
pull her back to a table
set with meat and potatoes

she grew tall eating white bread
smeared with butter and sugar
married a pragmatic man who worked hard
kept everything tidy but didn't know
who she was   they cried together
before she left on a Sunday's-child-is-full-of-woe-day

she packed bits of string, wood, dog fur,
and paper-white flower bulbs
she met a man who walked clouds
and etched them on glass
he wandered and wondered
so much he forgot her name sometimes

she moved away from him but still felt
his nimbus-cloud-walker-skin
under her eyelids and fingernails
she stared at night skies
and pulled trees in close
she simplified her collections

of rocks and broken eyeglasses
held in containers of painted tins
but she tripped in practical shoes
and lost her way on alphabetized-streets
she grew wrinkles that she liked to study
did yoga to imagine her back as an uncoiling cobra

she called the man to read poems aloud
he invited her to sit in hot baths
feeling age attaching to her limbs
she thought it might be good to drive
through the Plains once more
she knows they are anything

but plain and she might find
an elk femur or a day fresh
as one when she was small
and conversed often with a black Labrador
named T-Bone

Querencia

I

"Querencia"—
the place in the ring
where the bull centers himself
gathers each chest muscle firm
each hind quarter that quivers
not quite conscious   of who he is
but that he is ready   not yet knowing for what.

II

"Get ready, Baby"
"get ready" she said to her belly
as she walked from hospital parking
lot where she'd waited 'til after
midnight to save
on the cost of the coming.
In the dark and cushioned
walls of her womb, the babe pushed
headfirst into the bull-black
night in the month of May.

Sobremesa

pinon coffee pours into cups
a serum for truth or near truths
should a life story be told only once
to keep it honest
      no matter
someone reminds from the "Queen" to imagine
6 impossible things before breakfast
what have you dreamed?
I dreamed the baby girl's first words
came while sitting on my bed
she looked into my eyes and said "steel, stone, bone"
solid words from rosebud lips
      contradictions   contraindications   coincidences
existing in more than one world in more than one way
letting go of commands directives and yeah-buts
ahh the impossible possibilities we speak this day after breakfast
the taste of the eyes around the table make me lick my lips
I might swallow a whole lake if sipped daily
every cross or uncross of arms feels familiar
to each hair on my skin
is it my eyes or shadows blending space between
eyes   speckled arms   and four-chambered hearts
are the two dogs and one cat already here at this breakfast
or signs to come based on the configuration of potted plants
and assorted gatherings on the window sill
once I brought home the spine of an antelope carcass
one might get stiffer-backed as she grows old
or slip into other bodies more easily than ever

after Huevos Rancheros there's an easing into self
a newborn curling still present in the awakened
before the hardness of noon and the resolve of night

Svaha

He put her well-used rosary
and asthma inhaler in the urn
with her body's ashes and slivers
of bone   she who taught
that lightning whips the senses
and thunder asks, "What did you risk
with those in-between seconds?"

these short practices
for those other seconds
between becoming and dying
times to fill with   ritual   to bemoan   to rejoice

lightning reminds us we have
no power to stop what's coming
thunder reminds how it feels to be safe
safe as someone taking your body
out of the wet and cold
gathering you in a blanket of arms
adding warm words to caress

then the pouring of black tea
with time to reflect on every shade of blue ever felt
space between drips of slow honey
to consider every gasp you've ever gasped

Tingo

the neighbor comes for oranges to see what I might offer
I give him wooden fruit with a shrug
when he solicits conversation
I hand him a dictionary

I see meaning in his askings
so when he requests a pen
I give the one attached
to my thoughts

he asks for scissors
I fold my hair into his hands
he requests a washcloth
I give my morning scent

he asks for music
I hand over melodic sighs
and whispers in flute shapes
he inquiries about my heart

        I offer the whole beating mass

I watch from the window
as he carries wooden fruit
and a dictionary to a moving van
our homes so close I see sweat

drip down his neck
he carries a basin I bought in Mexico
the kind with flowers and skeletons
on a blue background

        something is pulsing in the basin

Glossary of Titles

Cafuné: Brazilian Portuguese—The act of tenderly running one's fingers through another's hair.

Culaccino: Italian—The mark left on a table by a cold glass.

Duende: Spanish—While originally used to describe a mythical, sprite-like entity that possesses humans and creates the feeling of awe of one's surroundings in nature, its meaning has transitioned into referring to "the mysterious power that a work of art has to deeply move a person."

Iktsuarpok: Inuit—To go outside to check if anyone is coming.

Jayus: Indonesian—A joke so poorly told and so unfunny that one cannot help but laugh.

Komorebi: Japanese—Sunlight filtering through the trees—the interplay between the light and the leaves. The first Japanese symbol is for tree, the second symbol means escape, and the third is for light or sun.

L'appel du vide: French—"The call of the void" is this French expression's literal translation, but more significantly it's used to describe the instinctive urge to jump from high places.

Litost: Czech—A state of agony and torment created by the sudden sight of one's own misery.

Nefelibata: Portuguese—dreamer, fantasizer, one who indulges in daydreams, cloud walker, one who lives in the clouds of the imagination.

Petrichor: Petra comes the Greek, *petra*, meaning "stone" + "ichor," the fluid that flows in the veins of the gods in Greek mythology.

Petrichor is an earthy scent produced when rain falls on dry soil. This word is not an untranslatable, but a newly coined word (1964) by Australian scientists.

Querencia: Spanish—from the Spanish verb "querer," which means "to desire." Querencia describes a place where one feels safe, a place from which one's strength of character is drawn, a place where one feels at home.

Sehnsucht: German—translated as "longing", "pining", "yearning", or "craving"or in a wider sense a type of "intensely missing".

Sobremesa: Spanish—the sociable time after a meal when you have food-induced conversations with the people you have shared the meal with.

Svaha: Origin unknown but believed by some to be a Native American word meaning the time between seeing the lightning and hearing the thunder, and also knowing what is coming but unable to stop it.

Tingo: Pascucense (Eastern Indonesian language spoken on Easter Island)—to gradually steal all the possessions out of a neighbor's house by borrowing and not returning.

Torschlusspanik: German—Literally translated, this word means "gate-closing panic," but its contextual meaning refers to "the fear of diminishing opportunities as one ages." Quote in this poem comes from Loren Eiseley

Ya'aburnee: Arabic—Both beautiful and morbid at the same time, this incantatory word means "You bury me," a declaration of one's hope that they'll die before another person because of how difficult it would be to live without them.

Mary Strong Jackson was born and raised in Western Nebraska with short but important periods in Washington and Oregon. As a social worker, Mary has worked in Nebraska, New Mexico, and England. Before getting her degree in social work and an MA in Education, she began writing poetry at her kitchen table, as a stay-at-home mother of three. Poetry transformed mundane daily chores into validations of her life. Her work has focused on adults, foster children, and their parents with diagnoses of mental illness. In her desire to give voice to those with mental illness, she collaborated with clients to create a book of prose and poetry, titled, *Singing Under Water.* Mary's poetry has appeared in journals and anthologies in the United States and England. Her chapbook titles are *The Never-Ending Poem, Witnesses, No Buried Dogs, Between Door and Frame,* and *Clippings.* She was included in a 2005 Nebraska Educational Television program featuring United States Poet Laureate, Ted Kooser. Mary resides in Appleton, Wisconsin.

www.ingramcontent.com/pod-product-compliance
Lightning Source LLC
LaVergne TN
LVHW041522070426
835507LV00012B/1747